Written By
Lashana Standard

Illustrated By
Whimsical Designs By CJ

Text © 2024 by Lashana Standard

Illustrations © 2024 by Whimsical Designs By CJ

All rights reserved. This book or any portion therefore may not be reproduced or used in any manner whatsoever without the express written permission of the publisher except for the use of brief quotations in a book review.

Printed in the United States of America

First Printing, 2025

ISBN: 9798315302643

To my son Tymeer,
my inspiration and greatest joy
—this is for you.

Chase will take you on another journey ride out of this world but this time through number space.

So hop on and take a fun ride with him on his rocket ship learning numbers 1-20.

Ready 5, 4, 3, 2, 1, Blast Off!

First we land on **Space 1**!

Hooray!

Where we count one astronaut floating.

No way!!

Next we ride to Space 2. Where we count two aliens playing with glue.

Would you like to play too?

Space 3. There are three giant milky ways.

Let's eat them for many days!

Now let's hurry to Space 4,
where we count four gorillas yelling.

What are they counting?

We almost missed Space 6 because it was raining six giant fruity pebbles.

Look out!! Now off to....

Space 7 is where we use seven telescopes to see the far away planets! Uh Oh one small planet is inside my jacket!

Count quickly!

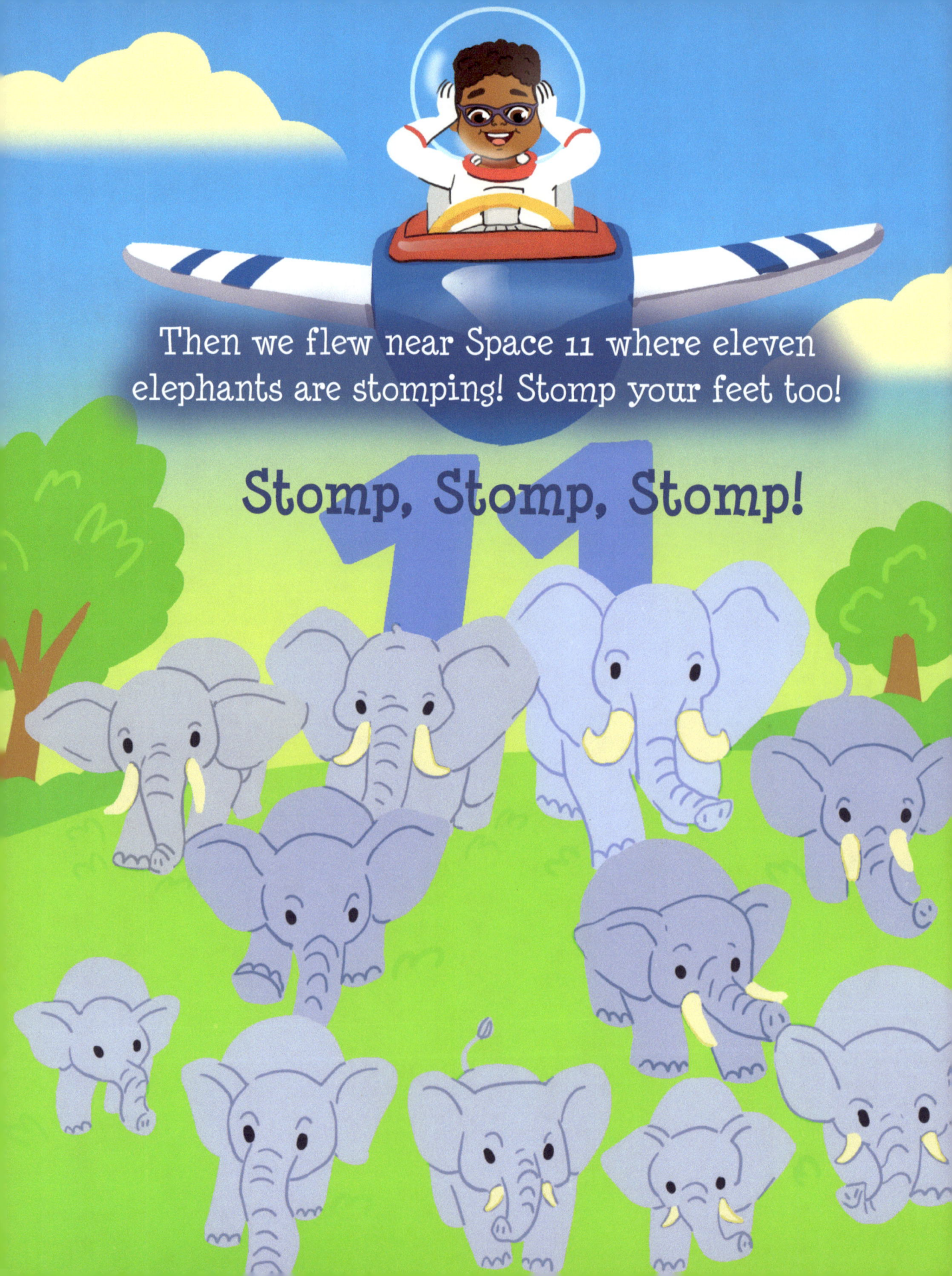

Then we flew near Space 11 where eleven elephants are stomping! Stomp your feet too!

Stomp, Stomp, Stomp!

Next we landed at Space 12, where twelve teddy bears are giving out big hugs.

Have you hugged someone today?

Next, we are headed to Space 13. Where we count thirteen bugs crawling around the sun!

Creepy!!

15

Now we are headed to Space 15!!
We count fifteen pigs eating ice.
Umm, that doesn't seem right!

At Space 18, we count eighteen cows jumping over the moon.

Oh that's so cool!

Then off to Space 19,
to count nineteen yellow marbles.

Last stop is Space 20, where we count twenty bouncy balls. Oh No, count fast before they fall!

If you want to take this fun ride again turn around and head back through Number Space 1-20.

The End

About the Author

Lashana Standard is a paraprofessional, a Child Development Specialist and a mother to four boys. Ms. Standard is dedicated to inspiring children to dream big and reach for opportunities beyond the roles most often talked about on career day at schools.

www.ingramcontent.com/pod-product-compliance
Lightning Source LLC
LaVergne TN
LVHW070434080526
838201LV00132B/274